A New Kind of Hustle

How to Find Success in the Midst of Obstacles

A TRUE STORY

> Dr. Lewis,
> "It is because of teachers like you that I can be the Doctor I am today."
>
> Michael D. Smith
> Doctor of Engineering

> Dr. Lewis,
> "You taught me to believe in myself and that it is okay to be different."
>
> Robert Shepard
> Public School Teacher

Sugar Lee Lewis, PhD

with Grace LaJoy Henderson, PhD

Inspirations by Grace LaJoy
Arlington, TX
www.gracelajoy.com
poetry@gracelajoy.com

Cover by Grace LaJoy Henderson
A New Kind of Hustle is a true story as told by Dr. Sugar Lee Lewis and written by Dr. Grace LaJoy Henderson

A NEW KIND OF HUSTLE: *How to find success in the midst of obstacles*
Copyright © 2013. Inspirations by Grace LaJoy
Published by Inspirations by Grace LaJoy
Arlington, TX 76096
www.gracelajoy.com

ISBN: 978-0-9829404-5-7

All rights reserved. No portion of this book may be printed, copied, reproduced or transmitted in any form without prior written permission from the publisher.

Printed in the United States of America

Praises for...
A NEW KIND OF HUSTLE:
How to find success in the midst of obstacles

"This story clearly demonstrates the importance of an education as a means to achievement. It could encourage some of those students who are faced with seemingly insurmountable odds to stay the course to graduation."

Doris Norvelle Briscoe, Director - Secondary Literacy
Fort Worth Independent School District

"It is a powerful personal story! The author paints a vivid picture of the obstacles she was determined to overcome."

Dr. Tammie Lovelady-Spain, Author
No Principal Left Behind
Former Public School Principal

"Dr. Sugar Lee Lewis's autobiography gave meaning to my life as it is told with a human spirit."

Dr. James A. Crawford
Doctor of Podiatric Medicine

Foreword

I truly believe that seeds of greatness are planted in every person, and that it is up to the individual to find the POWER that will allow those seeds of greatness to bring forth their destiny. Dr. Lewis's story of perseverance and creative ingenuity will help so many people gain self-esteem, inspiration and hope.

Charles M. Wolford II, Executive Director
The Turn-Around Agenda - Dallas, TX

Table of Contents

Introduction		1
Chapter 1	Hustling Through Poverty	3
Chapter 2	The Great Move	7
Chapter 3	Born to Hustle	11
Chapter 4	A Hustle of Our Own	13
Chapter 5	Hustling to Survive	17
Chapter 6	Hustling to Succeed	21
Chapter 7	Hustling to Stay Focused	27
Chapter 8	Hustling to Help Others	31
Conclusion		35
Discussion Questions		36
Questions Teachers Can Ask		38

INTRODUCTION

Drug dealers, pimps, bootleggers, thieves and those who sale stolen goods; These are the types of individuals who come to mind when we think of a hustler. In her new book, A NEW KIND OF HUSTLE, Dr. Sugar Lee Lewis redefines the word "hustler". After watching her parents and brothers hustle, Dr. Lewis developed a "hustle" of her own. As you read her fascinating story, you will find that she has been successful in her home, in school, with her family, on her job, in the community, and with business endeavors. These things represent her "hustle", which makes her the real deal!

You will also find that she has helped others to become hustlers as well. She has helped family members, community leaders, small business owners, non-profit executives, educators, and the list goes on.

One day Dr. Lewis was talking to two teenage young men, giving them insight on ways to be successful; after hearing her story of the challenges she faced growing up, one of the young men said to the other, "Now, that is what you call a true hustler." Her story empowered them both to believe that if she could "hustle" her way to success so could they.

Lots of people feel they don't have the ability to succeed or that the ability they have is not enough to reach success. Every child is born with the ability to succeed. There is a hustle in everyone, but, we all need something or someone to motivate us to move from one level to the next.

By nurturing and developing our hustle, we create the drive necessary to fuel our ability to reach success. This story is designed to let readers know that it doesn't matter where you begin reaching; as long as you begin somewhere and never give up.

Dr. Lewis is proof there is more than one type of hustler and there is more than one way to hustle. She has often said, "I'm on a mission, hustling to change the world one person at a time. I want to help as many people as I can as I travel through this world. " She has indeed hustled all her life; her empowering story will cause readers to say, in a positive sense, "I want to be a hustler" and "Teach me a new kind of hustle!"

Chapter 1: HUSTLING THROUGH POVERTY

Mom and Dad were hustlers! They grew up in an era in which slavery had just ended. Mom was never taught to read or write and Dad only had a third grade education, so his reading and writing skills were limited. Growing up in two very small rural towns in Louisiana, their homes did not have water, gas, or electricity. They did not even have an inside restroom! I remember my parents living this way even when I was a little girl.

To use the "toilet", we had to go outside to a little shack, which we called "the outhouse". Inside of the outhouse, was a hole that had been dug in the ground with boards on top of it, which was used like the toilets we have in our bathrooms today. The major difference between today's bathroom and an outhouse was that I had to take a broom to the outhouse to fight against the spider webs that had been built by big black spiders!

We were poor and did not have furniture. I slept on the floor and was afraid of the large rats that would crawl at night looking for food. I don't know how I made it through those very scary night nights. One night my feet were sticking out of the covers as my siblings and I slept on the floor. Suddenly a large rat crawled on top of my feet. I screamed, shook my foot intensely, and commanded the rat to get off my feet! As the rat ran away, I shook the cover to make sure there were no more rats, put the cover over my feet and went back to sleep. I don't think this was the lifestyle Mom and Dad envisioned for their family when they got married.

Mom grew up in Ada Taylor, Louisiana and Dad grew up in Ringgold, Louisiana. They got married at a very early age. Both were raised on farms, in which they raised all their own food. I saw chickens, cows, peach trees, plum trees, cherry trees, grapes, greens, peas, sweet potatoes, watermelon all in our yard! Today we call those types of foods "organic".

When I got hungry, I would go outside to the front of the house and pick fruit off the tree to eat. Oh, that fruit was so good! When I was thirsty, I went out to the well in the back of the house to get a drink of water. There was always a rope and a bucket on the well. I would release the bucket into the well, and pull the bucket back up with the rope and bring water back up in the bucket.

The good thing was that while we were outside playing, we did not have to go inside of the house to get a drink of water. We would just walk over to the well and get a drink! Because of the way my family and I ate and drank from the natural food and water from the great outdoors, none of us were ever overweight...and we hardly ever got sick. In fact, I did not see many unhealthy people back in those days.

I learned a lot from Mom and Dad. Even when they did not have the luxury of water, gas, and electricity...and even though they were poor, they took what they had and used it to survive. They were true hustlers! They took eggs, which came from their chickens, and milk and butter which came from their cows, and traded them for things that they needed.

One day, Mom and Dad when out into the yard and gathered some eggs that had been laid by one of their chickens. They took the eggs down the road and traded them for some of Aunt Lou's vegetables. Aunt Lou needed the eggs to finish making her cake. Mom and dad needed the vegetables for next week's dinner. There was never any exchange of money when items were traded.

For money, my parents went to the cotton field and picked cotton. With the money they earned, they bought things like flour and clothes... things that could not be grown in their yard. They also used the money they earned to help others. One day, as I was walking through the living room to go into the kitchen, I saw Aunt Doll, my mother's youngest sister, in the living room talking with Mom and Dad.

Aunt Doll helped around the house daily and watched the children while all of Mom's other siblings worked in the field. Since Aunt Doll was unable to work in the field to earn money, Mom and Dad gave her some money to buy flour and material. This is just one of the many examples of how I saw my parents help other people.

Mom and Dad did not have much during this time, but, they always dreamed of having a better life for themselves. More so, they wanted all of their children to have much more in life than they did, which led to the great move.

Chapter 2: THE GREAT MOVE

I was seven years old when Mom and Dad packed up me, my three older brothers, my baby sister, and everything we owned and moved to Barstow, California. This great move happened at a time when Mom and Dad had given birth to eight children and lost three to death. This was a challenging time for them, but, they had high hopes for better opportunities for our family.

Dad chose California because the state was not segregated like Louisiana. Segregation means that African American (black) people did not have the same privileges as Caucasian (white) people. They could not attend the same schools, restaurants, parks, movies, or even drink from the same water fountain!

The number one reason for the great move to California is that Mom and Dad did not want us to grow up in a segregated state. They wanted us to have beds and to know how to read and write. Dad felt that, in Louisiana, blacks would never have the opportunity to do much more than pick cotton. He felt like there was no concern about whether black families learned to read or write or if they had a good life.

The number two reason why Mom and Dad moved to California is because Dad's sister and brother, Aunt Maxine and Uncle Shed lived in California. Uncle Shed worked for the Santa Fe Railroad. Aunt Maxine's husband, Uncle General, worked for the railroad also. They were not poor like we were, and every one of their children were enrolled in school and were learning how to read and write. They all had beds, too!

As soon as we moved to Barstow, Dad was offered a job as a fork-lifter for the United States Marine Corp Supply Center. He accepted the job immediately and worked there until he retired. Dad told me that a fork-lift is a machine that lifts heavy boxes, equipment, and other things that are too heavy to lift with your hands.

When we got to Barstow, Mom did not work on a job, she was a stay-at-home mom. She never even learned how to drive a car. She was a caretaker. She cared for us and other children in the neighborhood while their parents worked. She volunteered to help those who were sick by taking them food and caring for them in their homes.

One day Mom's best friend, Miss Lackey, was sick. Mom cooked for her, cleaned her house, and made sure her children got on the bus to go to school. Mom did the same thing for Miss King, who lived across the street from us. Mom volunteered in the community, cleaned the streets, and she never asked for any money for her services. She brought the southern Louisiana hospitality to the state of California!

In California, my siblings and I finally got a chance to go to school like everyone else! I remember the first day we went to school. "We're going to school tomorrow!" I told my brothers. I was so excited the night before, that I could not even sleep! Mom woke us up out of our *beds*, which we did not have before the great move. "Everybody get up and get ready for school!" she said. My heart was full of joy as I hopped out of bed and ran to the kitchen table for breakfast.

Mom had cooked biscuits, eggs, and salt pork, which is kind of like bacon. Then we washed it all down with a cold glass of milk. After breakfast, I hurried to get dressed and went out to the bus stop. Mom came out the bus stop to make sure our hair was still in place, no food was on our mouths, and our faces were greased with petroleum jelly, and that we had not gotten our clothes dirty.

Mom did not want us to go to our first day of

school in Barstow dressed any old kind of way. Even though all of our clothes were used, we dressed up like we were going to a special event. Mom made the girls wear dresses and Dad made the boys where slacks. The petroleum jelly was to protect our skin from the sun, but, we were teased by classmates because of our shiny faces. The teasing made me feel embarrassed, but, I just smiled and moved on. My brothers and sisters just laughed it off, too. We were so excited to be going to school that being teased did not really bother us.

    This great move caused a special bond between me, my younger sister, and my three brothers. Instead of working in the cotton field the way we did in Louisiana, we actually had a chance to have fun together and to do things like talk and play. We even walked to the school bus stop together. My brothers and I watched as Mom and Dad hustled from poverty to a better life.

Chapter 3: BORN TO HUSTLE

I was born in Ringgold, Louisiana on May 28, 1945. Mom told me I was the smallest child born to them and that I was lucky to have survived. I was so small that my family gave me the nick name, Teeny. Dad named me Sugar Lee, after my mother. He said it was because he loved her so much that he wanted me to have the same name as her.

Mom agreed to name me Sugar because I survived at birth; and with so many baby girls dying at birth, my mom thought I should have a "sweet" name.

I was the seventh child born. Before Mom and Dad gave birth to me, they had given birth to six other children. The first born was my brother "Sugar B" who died at birth.

The second born was my sister Mattie, who was named after my grandmother. She died at birth, too. The third born was my sister Willie Mae, who died at twelve years old. I was a little girl, about two or three years old, when she died. A splinter got into her hand and she got blood poisoning which caused her death. The fourth, fifth, and sixth born where my three brothers, Ben, Paul, and John; I was the seventh and my baby sister Mary Louise was the eighth.

I learned a lot from watching Mary Louise. She graduated from high school and worked on various types of jobs. She was multi-talented! She and her husband of forty years raised five children together. I admired her as she embraced her role as wife and mother. She hustled to make sure the needs of her family were met. Like Mom, Mary was *always* helping people.

Before Mary Louise was born, I was the only girl living in a house with three boys. I learned the most from my brothers during that time. My brothers often talked about current events. They enjoyed science, math, repairing cars, and playing sports. Being around them cause me to like all of those same things.

While other girls played soft games like tennis and table games, I played rough sports like football. Girls would say to me, "You're not supposed to do that, that's what boys do!" Well, being the only girl in a house with all boys, I didn't know the difference. Being born in a house with all boys automatically taught me to hustle harder than the average girl!

Chapter 4: A Hustle of Our Own

I watched the way Mom and Dad trained my brothers and instilled in them the importance of work. I admired my brothers and wanted to do whatever they did. Where ever they were was where I wanted to be!

My brothers, Ben, Paul, and John were born in the 1940's at a time when it was becoming increasingly more important for young men to be educated. But, my brothers took it a step further, not only did Ben and Paul become complete high school and some college, they became great business men, too! But, John had special needs and was limited to how far he could strive.

All three shined shoes and delivered papers when they were young. All loved people just like Mom and Dad. They were helpers and always did things for others as little boys and as they grew older. I often saw Paul helping friends who were in need. He let them lived with him in his house, he gave them jobs in his business, he gave them clothes, cars, and money! He had a great big heart!

Ben was multi-talented. He worked with his hands and, during high school, he repaired cars with dad. By his senior year, Ben had secured a job on the

Marine Corp base. He also had a paper route, which eventually became very large. He delivered the daily newspaper to the entire city and I helped!

I would get up early in the morning, in extremely hot weather, to roll papers, put rubber bands around them, and load them into the car. He drove while I sat in the back seat and threw the papers, out of the car window, into the yards.

Ben later started his own business by buying three trailers. He lived in one and rented the other two out. His hard work allowed him to buy a home in his early thirties. When I turned sixteen, Ben helped me get a job in the cafeteria on the Marine Corp base. He helped Paul get a job there, too!

While working in the cafeteria on the base, Paul learned how to make sandwiches. He used what he learned from the cafeteria to start a catering business out of a truck. At the time he was the only black-owned catering business in the community. He had a mini store in his truck! He delivered sandwiches, sodas, potato chips, cookies, candy, and gum to construction sites and they purchased from him. He used the money he earned to buy himself a house and to help me go to college.

While Ben and Paul both knew the importance of education, John became known as the alcoholic of the family. He eventually ended up on receiving disability payments because he was diagnosed with a mental condition called retardation. He never learned to read and did not finish high school. Back then, special education programs were not available in schools the way they are today. By watching John, I learned what *not* to do. I only wish more help would have been available to him.

I helped John a lot until he died at age sixty-six. When John was forty-five years old, I took him on a trip to a place in the mountains, called Calico Ghost Town. While there, I took all kinds of photos of him and made a photo book of pictures of only him. When I gave it to him, he cried. He said no one had ever taken that type of interest to do such a wonderful thing for him. John's appreciation for what I did encouraged me to want to help other people.

Overall, I made sure John had everything he needed. Even though his ability was limited, *he* was a hustler also! I watched as he waved people down as they walked down the street, asking, "Hey, would you like to have your shoes shined?" We each developed our own hustle to survive!

Chapter 5: Hustling to Survive

The great move initially provided a sense of security for our family. We went from sleeping on cold wooden floors to having warm beds to sleep in. We went from picking cotton to going to school. We went from being segregated to being free. But, sadly we still lived in poverty and had to hustle to survive. Life seemed great for a few months, but, then reality set in.

As a child I did not like myself very much. I was often bullied and ridiculed for having skinny legs, short hair, smelling badly, and wearing dirty clothes. Teachers felt sorry and took a special interest in me. One day I came to school and Miss Sawyer said to me, "baby, you smell like pee". Then she took me by the hand and walked me to the nurse's office, cleaned me up, and gave me some clean clothes to wear. I felt good for the rest of the day.

But, even on the days when I felt clean, I still felt dumb. I felt like everyone in my class was much smarter than me, especially when the teacher would have us do "mental math". Miss Weatherby would place us in two teams. Each student in each group would have to answer a math question without using pencil and paper. Everyone would answer correctly except me. I *always* needed assistance to answer my mental math problem.

Whereas my classmates got assistance with homework at home, my parents were unable to help me because they never learned to read or write. However, there was a lot of concern about education in my neighborhood. Our principal Miss McKinney would bring teachers, drive down my street, and ask if we needed help with homework.

Miss McKinney had the insight to see that we needed help with school work. But, what she did *not* know was that we often had no food in our house. She didn't know Mom often dug through garbage, in back of grocery stores and restaurants, for bruised fruit just so we could have something to eat. She didn't know I killed pigeons, cooked them, and ate them... or that I dug through garbage for food, just like Mom.

One day I was really hungry. So, I walked to Hardwick Grocery Store, went over to the garbage can, and took out bruised apples, bananas, grapes and even meat. I saw flies, fruit flies, and pigeons flying around over the garbage can. But, I continued to dig out the fruit and meat because I was so hungry and wanted something to eat.

I knew the food in the garbage was old and outdated but, at the time, I didn't know the dangers of eating out of the trash can. I ate the fruit, but, took the meat home to Mom and she cooked it for the family. In exchange for food, Mom helped our neighbor, Miss Mattie Davis, with her children. To help feed the family, Dad would take a large tub to a bread truck and fill it with outdated bread for one dollar.

During the winter holiday, a great big truck came through the neighborhood and brought fresh food and toys to the house! Although we lived in the suburbs in a newer house, and Dad was employed, we still struggled. This, along with the bullying I endured, made me not like myself much.

By the time I entered high school, I began to like myself a little more. During this time, I took a home economics class and learned how to make clothes for myself. Making my own clothes caused me to look and feel better. I also took business classes and learned how to apply for a job, fill out income tax forms, and how to type on a typewriter.

I became an office helper and participated in multiple school activities like athletics, choir, drill team, newspaper editor, and Future Nurses of America. I became the first black person to compete for Miss Barstow for the city of Barstow in California.

Perhaps the greatest accomplishment as a young person was the day I came up with an idea for my classmates and I to walk from Barstow to Victorville, California, which was a thirty mile walk. Out of twelve people only one person completed the walk and it was me! News reporters covered the story and for the first time in my life, my name was in the news headlines, "Sugar Lee Hamptlon completes thirty mile walk to Victorville, California". Survival of the hard times led to a continual hustle to succeed.

Chapter 6: HUSTLING TO SUCCEED

After high school, I attended college at Grambling State University for one year. Then I married Mr. Luster. We were married for five years and had three children together. We have six grand children and two great grand children.

My first born was Michelle, who was very creative and artistic. She was the reader of the family and a good writer. In school she played the violin in the orchestra and the clarinet in the school band. She was multi-talented, studied multiple topics in college, and used her skills to secure various types of jobs. Michelle never had any children.

My second born was Yolanda, who loved science and math. She played the cello and saxophone in the school band. She studied engineering in college and became a mechanical engineer for Ford Motor Company. She also earned a Master's Degree in Business Administration (MBA) and eventually became a Lieutenant Colonel for the United States Army. Yolanda was shot in Bagdad, Iraq and was awarded the Purple Heart, Bronze Star, and the Combat Action Badge. She had two children, Cheyenne and Brandon.

Cheyenne speaks Spanish fluently, plays the trumpet and cello, and is an expert at playing Chess. As a freshman in high school, she began making plans to attend college to earn a degree in mechanical engineering. Brandon also speaks Spanish fluently and plays the saxophone. He, too, is a Chess expert! He enjoys playing football, basketball and soccer. As a sixth grader in middle school, he began making plans to go to college to study engineering.

My third born was Elroy, just like Yolanda, he loved math and science. In school, he played the viola in the orchestra. He also played basketball and football. In college, he majored in Engineering and worked multiple types of jobs. He had four children, Demetra, Roy, Shelby, and Elroy III.

Deme'tra graduated from high school and earned a Cosmetology License. Then she enrolled in college to study to become a Medical Assistant. Roy became an air plane pilot at the age of 15! In school, he played football, basketball, and the saxophone. After graduating from high school, Roy went to college to study Architectural Engineering.

Shelby earned a Certified Nursing Assistant Certificate while still in high school! After high school graduation, she went to college to study to become a Nurse Anesthetist. Elroy III played football and basketball in high school. He also played the trumpet in high school band. During high school, Elroy III made the decision to go to college to become a Lawyer.

My two great granddaughters are R'mani and Jaidense. As preschoolers, we began instilling in them the importance of completing high school and college.

I was pregnant with Elroy when my husband had a massive heart attack and died. Michelle was only four years old and Yolanda was three. Suddenly, I became the sole provider for my three children. It was tough, but, I hustled to give them everything I did not have growing up. I went to all of their school activities, traveled with them, and encouraged them to get involved with community service.

Going to college was not an option! I automatically instilled that in my children. They automatically knew, without question, that after graduating high school, college was the next step.

Everything Mom and Dad did not do with me, I did with my children. I did not have anyone to help me with my homework, so I made sure I always helped them with theirs. I made sure my children were always clean, wore clean clothes, and never *ever* had to eat out of a garbage can!

During this very challenging time of my life, I enrolled at Barstow Community College and earned an Associate's degree. While I was taking courses, the dean of the college encouraged me to complete my education. "Your children will need a role model. They will need someone to look up to and respect. Finishing your college education will have an impact on their lives."

So, after I completed my Associate's degree, I transferred to the University of Missouri - Kansas City, where I completed my Bachelor's degree. I had a goal to not get married until I completed my education, so after I completed my Bachelor's degree, I remarried.

The degree enabled me to secure a job as a teacher for the Kansas City, Missouri School District, where I met Miss Ellison. It wasn't long before she became my mentor. She encouraged me to go to every professional development workshop that the school district offered. She also encouraged me to continue on to earn my Master's degree.

Miss Ellison only had her Bachelor's degree and suffered regrets that she had never taken her education any further. So, she did not want me to make the same mistake she made by not securing her Master's degree. With Miss Ellison's encouragement, I completed my Master's and Educational Specialist degrees while enduring numerous struggles. My second marriage ended in a divorce after twenty years.

With all of the adversity I endured while caring for a husband, raising children, working, and pursuing higher education, I struggled to stay focused to continue moving forward.

Chapter 7: Hustling to Stay Focused

After I completed my Education Specialist degree, my focus was to help more people. To do that, my goal was to move into higher positions in the school district. Being an elementary teacher, I was limited to only helping the twenty children in my classroom. As vice principal and principal, I would be able to help the total staff *and* students. As a district administrator, I would have the power to help the entire school district! I knew I would have to stay focused to reach this goal.

My first year as a teacher I taught in the regular classroom. But, the next thirteen years I served as a gifted and talented teacher. One year I taught a set of identical twin boys. I could not tell them apart except by the expression on their faces. One of the twins exhibited confidence in himself and often wore a smile on his face.

The other twin exhibited a lack of confidence and often expressed sadness on his face. They both loved games and were fun to have in class. Sometimes they would sit in each other's desk on purpose just to trick me. I would talk to one and think I was talking to the other. When they realized I had fallen for their trick, they would laugh. It was always refreshing to see the "sad" twin laughing.

I had much success as a teacher, a vice principal, then a principal. I reached my ultimate goal of becoming an administrator in the school district's central office, where I finally reached my goal of helping the entire school district! As a Central Office Administrator, I worked in every single department in the district.

While working as a Human Resources (HR) Administrator, I found that many employees working in the HR Department only had high school level education. To help them to move ahead, I encouraged them to go to college.

One young lady who worked in the HR Department had lots of college credits, but, no degree. I knew the school district would be cutting back on staff and was looking to get rid of people who did not have degrees. So, I encouraged her to get her Bachelor's degree.

She took my advice and two months after she completed the degree, I receive a phone call from her. With teary eyes, she thanked me for encouraging her to complete her education. She told me that everyone in her department, who did not have a college degree, had been terminated! As a result of earning the degree, she still had her job!

I also found that many of the employees who *had* completed higher education needed education in a different field in order to move up at the school district. So, while encouraging them, I found myself inspired to go back to college to obtain my Doctorate's degree.

Over the years, I had the opportunity to help a lot of employees. I also helped many parents. One day a pregnant parent came into my office crying. She told me the story of how her child had been suspended from school and she didn't have anywhere for him to go while she worked. She was afraid of what could happen to him on the streets if he remained out of school.

I listened to her story, then I contacted a principal at a different school, shared with him the mother's concerns, and he allowed her son to enroll in his school. My goal was to prevent him from dropping out of school.

As soon as she left my office, she went into labor, went to the hospital, had a little girl...and named her Sugar! But, more importantly, she came into my office two years later and told me her son had finished high school. She thanked me and told me I saved her son's life!

I was not satisfied with merely *my own* success. In order to feel totally successful, I needed to help others also. I felt good knowing someone had a better life because of something I did. So, I continued my hustle to help others.

Chapter 8: HUSTLING TO HELP OTHERS

Eventually, I retired from the Kansas City, Missouri School District. It was during retirement that I made the decision to help as many people as I could before I leave this earth. I felt that I had been fortunate enough to be smart, talented, and successful. So, with no motive and wanting nothing in return, I set out to help as many people as possible.

I had already helped my children and grandchildren, students, educators, and parents. Now, I wanted to help gifted and talented adults who needed help pursuing their dreams and goals; who were aiming for success, but, had not quite reached it yet. *Their* success was *my* success!

I have helped executive directors form non-profit organizations and get grant money to finance their worthy cause. I have assisted business owners with reaching the next level in their business endeavors. But, perhaps the most memorable experience was when I encouraged an author, named Grace LaJoy, to write a book entitled, A Gifted Child in Foster Care.

Grace LaJoy and I met when we both served as administrators for the Kansas City Missouri School District. She left the school district and I had not seen her in several years. While walking through an exhibit hall at a school district event, I saw her again. She was one of the vendors, selling books, in the exhibit hall. Her books were spread out on her table. I was amazed to find out she had become an author of several books since leaving the school district! I never knew she was a gifted writer.

I asked her what made her start writing. She said her gift of writing stemmed from her mother leaving her, never to return, when she was only two years old. She would write to deal with her pain and feelings of rejection. She told me part of her childhood was spent living in a foster home. I was shocked to learn of her unfortunate background!

When Grace LaJoy and I worked together, she was bright, intelligent, respectable, and got along well with her co-workers. So, I never would have imagined that she would have gone through such a heart-breaking experience as a child. But, the part of her story that amazed me the most was she was actually placed in her school's gifted and talented program while living in the foster home!

Inspired by her story, I challenged her to write another book and give it the title, "A Gifted Child in

Foster Care". She took my advice and one year later she called me and told me she had written the rough draft of the book. I immediately went over to her house, read the rough draft, gave my input on what needed to be done to the book to ensure her story helps as many people as possible. She applied all of my suggestions, got input from others, and now her story, "A Gifted Child in Foster Care: A Story of Resilience", is being read in schools all over the United States!

Even though I reached success and helped others to do the same, I lacked in the self-confidence needed to keep myself encouraged. I was able to help bring out gifts and talents in others, but, there were still gifts and talents in myself that I need someone to help me to bring out. For example, writing my own life story.

After helping others, I wanted to write my story, but, did not have the creative skills necessary to put my story on paper. So, after I helped Grace LaJoy maximize her gifts and talents, she turned around and helped me to maximize mine! I encouraged her to writer *her* story, then she ended up helping me to write *mine*! I don't claim to know it all, but, that which I know I will share it with anyone at anytime.

We can help others, but, sometimes we need help. I believe that the more we hustle to help others, the more people will hustle to help us.

CONCLUSION

Perhaps the greatest lessons Sugar Lee learned were from her parents; being able to observe all the love her Mom and Dad showed towards others. They loved and helped everyone and they taught her how to love and help everyone, too. They did not just hustle for themselves and their family, but, to help others, too.

Sugar Lee's hustle caused her to be a woman of great influence and caused others to hustle, too. With education, she was able to buy the home she wanted, the care she desired, and several real estate properties, which she rents out to help other people. She was also able to take care of her mother until her mother died at ninety-six years old.

She got hers, then helped others to get theirs...giving the word "hustle" a new meaning. If you desire to succeed, and help other do the same, then education is the key:

- Attend school everyday
- Learn all you can
- Graduate from high school
- Pursue and complete college education

If you don't know where to begin, then it's time for you to learn A NEW KIND OF HUSTLE!

Discussion Questions

Note: *Read the entire book for enjoyment before beginning the discussion questions.*

These questions are designed to reinforce <u>eight</u> key reading comprehension skills.

- Think about the question
- Reread the chapter, if necessary
- Write your answer on a separate sheet of paper
- Discuss your answers

Chapter 1: HUSTLING THROUGH POVERTY
Theme/Concept

In what ways does the author address the concepts of poverty, healthy eating, and bartering?

Chapter 2: THE GREAT MOVE
Cause and Effect

What caused The Great Move? What effects did The Great Move have on the author and her family?

Chapter 3: BORN TO HUSTLE
Sequencing/Classifying

List the order of birth of the author and her siblings from youngest to oldest. Then classify your list into two categories.

Chapter 4: A Hustle of Our Own
Details

List all the details in Chapter 3 that the author provides about her brothers' knowledge, skills and talents.

Chapter 5: Hustling to Survive
Inference

Did the author provide a better life for her children than the she had growing up? What evidence supports your answer?

Chapter 6: Hustling to Succeed
Paraphrasing

In five sentences or less, describe the author's feelings about college.

Chapter 7: Hustling to Stay Focused
Summarizing

In your own words, summarize how the author helped others.

Chapter 8: Hustling to Help Others
Literary Elements

Do you think, as the author does, that "the more we hustle to help others, the more people will hustle to help us"? Why or why not?

Questions Teachers Can Ask
Critical Thinking/In-depth Comprehension/Writing Skills/Technology Skills

1. What is the Main ideal or Learning Experience of the book?

2. Write your thoughts or feelings about the story or your favorite character.

3. Summarize your favorite part of the book and tell why this was your favorite part.

4. Write about an experience in your personal life and tell how it is similar to this story.

5. Write a new summary of the book.

6. Write a new ending or a sequel chapter of the book.

7. Would you recommend this book? Why or Why not?

8. How can the information in the story be useful in your life or future?

9. Research a famous or infamous person on the computer and write a report about that person's life.

www.ingramcontent.com/pod-product-compliance
Lightning Source LLC
Chambersburg PA
CBHW071846290426
44109CB00017B/1943